The Bilbao Consulate and its Ordinances

Basque Politics Series No. 18

The Bilbao Consulate and its Ordinances:

The Tenacity of the Captains, Shipmasters, Merchants and Traders of Bilbao

Margarita Serna Vallejo

University of Cantabria

Center for Basque Studies Press
University of Nevada, Reno
2021

The Bilbao Consulate and its Ordinances:

The Tenacity of the Captains, Shipmasters, Merchants and Traders of Bilbao

The publisher gratefully acknowledges the generous contribution to this book provided by the Government of Bizkaia.

Series: Basque Politics Series No. 18

Series editor: Xabier Irujo

ISBN-10: 194980545X

ISBN-13: 978-1-94-980545-1

Library of Congress Cataloging in Publication Data

Names: Serna Vallejo, Margarita, author.
Title: The Bilbao consulate and its ordinances : the tenacity of the captains, shipmasters, merchants, and traders of Bilbao / by Margarita Serna Vallejo.
Description: Reno : University of Nevada, Center for Basque Studies, 2020.| Series: Basque politics series ; 15 | Includes bibliographical references.
Identifiers: LCCN 2021017163 | ISBN 9781949805451 (trade paperback)
Subjects: LCSH: Spain. Ordenanzas de la ilustre Universidad y Casa de Contratación de la M.N. y M.L. Villa de Bilbao. | Universidad y Casa de Contratación de la M.N. y M.L. Villa de Bilbao. Ordenanzas. | Foreign trade regulation--Spain--History. | Maritime law--Spain--History. | Commercial law--Spain--History.
Classification: LCC KKT3405 .S47 2020 | DDC 343.4608/7--dc23
LC record available at https://lccn.loc.gov/2021017163

Contents

The Framework in which the Consulate of Bilbao Was Founded:

The Hispanic Monarchy's Consular Institutions

Understanding the foundation of the Consulate of Bilbao in 1511 requires taking into account the context in which the Castilian crown decided to set it up and the situation of the consulates which by that date already existed within the framework of the Hispanic monarchy. Only in that context is it possible to assess to what extent the foundation of the Bilbao Consulate meant continuity or novelty within the peninsular consular tradition. At the same time, the notable changes that were incorporated into some consulates must be examined, as must the foundation of new consulates in the eighteenth century, to be able to correctly evaluate the importance of the renewal of the Consulate of Bilbao ordinances in 1737. These were the regulations by which the institution carried out its work in the final stage of its existence, which lasted until 1829, at which time all the consulates inherited from the Old Regime were replaced by the new commercial courts at the same time as the first commercial code came into force.

Before we pay attention strictly to the foundation of the Consulate of Bilbao at the beginning of the sixteenth century, and its ordinances, it is worth examining both the Hispanic consular cycles (to determine, as mentioned before, the context of the Bizkaian institution) and the first consular institution of the Crown of Castile, the Consulate of Burgos. There are three reasons for examining the latter. Firstly, the foundings of the Castilian consulates in Burgos and Bilbao were influenced by the commercial rivalry that had existed between the two cities and their merchants since the fifteenth century, which is why the institutionalization of both consulates must be explained in the context of this confrontation. Secondly, the Burgos commercial organization was the point of reference for founding the Consulate of Bilbao and was to become less important because of the foundation of the latter. Thirdly, immediately after the founding of the Burgos consulate, various decisions were taken by the Bilbao city council, its merchants, and the monarchy, all of which laid the foundations for the definitive and effective institutionalization of the Consulate of Bilbao in 1511.

The Hispanic Consular Cycles

The foundation of consulates by the Crown of Castile, including the Consulate of Bilbao, took place later than when the consulates of the Crown of Aragon, the oldest in the Iberian Peninsula, were established. So, while the eastern kingdoms on the Mediterranean already had practically all their consular institutions by the late Middle Ages, Castile's first consulate on the peninsula,[1]

---

1   Prior to the establishment of the Consulate of Burgos, the Consulate of Bruges had been founded outside the Iberian Peninsula, dependent on the Holy Spirit of Burgos brotherhood or university of merchants. That was the organization from which the initiative that finally led to the foundation of the consulate of Burgos was to emerge. The foundation of the Consulate of Bruges took place in 1428. However, in 1455, as a consequence of the confrontations between the Burgos consuls in Bruges and the shipmasters

in Burgos, was founded at the end of that period, in 1494.[2] The next, in Bilbao, was founded in 1511.[3] And later on there were consulates founded in Seville (1543),[4] and in Donostia in 1682.[5] In the peninsula, therefore, the consulates of the Crowns of Castile and Aragon only existed at the same time after 1494 and throughout the sixteenth and seventeenth centuries. In the eighteenth century it is no longer possible to differentiate between Castilian and Aragonese consulates. after the victory of Felipe V in the War of Succession, and the passing of *Nueva Planta* decrees, both the Crown of Aragon, and the four kingdoms it was composed of (Aragon, Valencia, Catalonia, and Mallorca), disappeared. Furthermore, the consulates which

---

of Bilbao, the institution was divided in two, giving rise to the Consulate of the "Nation" of Castile and the Consulate of the "Nation" of Bizkaia, to which both the Gipuzkoans and the people of Araba also belonged, especially people from Vitoria-Gasteiz. See Basas Fernández, 1963: 31-33; Coronas González, 1979: 81-129; García Fernández, 2005: 287-288; and González Arce, 2009: 80-81, and 2010.

2 Law of July 21, 1494. In García de Quevedo, 1905: 153-162.

3 Law of June 22, 1511. In *Prematicas, ordanças*, 1552.

4 Provision of August 23, 1543. In *Ordenanzas para el prior y cónsules*, 1739: 4-12.

5 Law of March 13, 1682. In *Consulado, y Casa de la Contratación*, 1714: 3-16.

were founded or reformed thereafter must be seen as consulates of the Spanish monarchy, and not as institutions belonging to each of the old crowns, especially considering the tendency toward homogenization.

The simultaneous existence (in the sixteenth and seventeenth centuries) of the consulates of the Crowns of Aragon and Castile—which, together, made up the Hispanic monarchy— does not mean that the consulates of both kingdoms followed the same model. Moreover, not even those of the same tradition always conformed to the same scheme, which is why there are significant variations among the consulates of each of the two crowns. This makes it necessary to differentiate two cycles in the history of Hispanic consulates. On the one hand, there were the Aragonese crown consulates of medieval origin, some of which continued to function until the beginning of the eighteenth century. On the other hand, the Castilian consulates started at the end of the fifteenth century and were open throughout the following two centuries.[6]

---

6   García Sanz, 1969: 226.

This structure would be incomplete, however, if a third cycle were not added: the consulates of the eighteenth century. These include, firstly, those consulates made official for the first time in this period following new guidelines which allowed for a Bourbon consular model. Secondly, we consider some consulates founded over the preceding centuries which, at the time of the eighteenth century, were remodelled in depth to adapt them to the new Bourbon model. And, finally, we add to this third cycle the Consulate of Bilbao, an institution which, thanks to the reform of its ordinances in 1737, among other circumstances, adapted to the Enlightenment but retained the fundamental features that it had had from its foundation, thus avoiding being adapted to the structure of the Bourbon consulates and, above all, disappearance—a possibility that some authorities close to the Monarchy seem to have considered at the beginning of the eighteenth century.[7]

---

7   The opinion of Fortún Íñiguez de Acurio given to Juan de Dios González de los Ríos, Marquis of Campoflorido, on the closure of the Consulate of Bilbao (January 1719). The text is published in Zabala y Allende, 1907: 98-100.

Finally, before proceeding further, we should point out that the differences between the various consulates of the monarchy as a whole until the beginning of the eighteenth century affected the two features which made up all the consulates.[8] *Lonja, universidad, cofradía,* or *casa de contratación de mercaderes*: several different names—in some cases at the same time—were used to describe the professional groups of merchants around which each of the consulates based its work. As for the second essential and characteristic feature of all consulates, there were the consular courts. If these consular courts were not founded within the framework of a group of merchants, it would not have been possible to speak of the existence of a consular institution.[9]

The Crown of Aragon's Medieval Consulates: From Maritime Consulates to Commercial Consulates

The origin of the maritime consulates of the Crown of Aragon dates to the thirteenth century

---

8   Smith, 1978: 17.

9   Gacto Fernández, 1971: 29.

and, particularly, to the fourteenth, when the Aragonese monarchy made most of its consulates official and reorganized or reopened some institutions that had existed previously, adjusting them to this new consular situation.

In Valencia the consulate was established in 1283;[10] in Mallorca in 1326;[11] in Barcelona the old consulate was reformed in 1348 to fit in with the Mallorca consulate model;[12] in Tortosa, in 1363, the post of maritime and fluvial consuls, that had existed since 1248, was also reformulated in order to adapt it to the structure of the Consulate of Mallorca;[13] in Gerona it was founded in 1385;[14] in Perpignan it was opened in 1388;[15] and in San Feliu de Guíxols it was founded in 1443.[16] Only the foundation of the Consulate of Lleida

---

10 Privilege of December 1, 1283. In Serna Vallejo, 2018a: 18-19.

11 Privilege of February 1, 1326. In Serna Vallejo, 2018a: 19-20.

12 Privilege of February 20, 1348. In Serna Vallejo, 2018a: 21-22.

13 Privilege of July 23, 1363. In Serna Vallejo, 2018a: 23-24.

14 Privilege of October 14, 1385. In Serna Vallejo, 2018a: 24-26.

15 Privilege of December 22, 1388. In Serna Vallejo, 2018a: 27-28.

16 Privilege of February 11, 1443. In Serna Vallejo, 2018a: 28-30.

was delayed until the beginning of the modern era, specifically until 1510.[17]

Although practically all these consulates were founded in the late Middle Ages, they were not the same in type or structure. And what is more relevant, they did not take on the same roles either. Furthermore, throughout this period most of the consulates were dynamic institutions which changed in type and roles over time.

The oldest consulates founded in the Crown of Aragon in the late Middle Ages were set up as maritime consulates in the strict sense, which explains that from early on they were called "sea consulates," while, to the contrary, most of those created in the following phase, although also in the late medieval period, were founded as mercantile consulates.

The consulates in the second stage were set up as mercantile institutions, having authority over both terrestrial and maritime trade despite their nomenclature as maritime consulates. They were given the same nomencla-

---

17 Privilege of June 30, 1510. In Mut Remola, 1952: 72-73.

ture which the old consulates had been given, although the latter, originally, had been exclusively maritime consulates, with authority over only maritime trade. Over the passage of time, however, they, too, had become mercantile in terms of their scope of activity, although without having changed their nomenclature to reflect that change.

The composition of the social basis for these consulates, the competences they received from the monarchy at the time of their foundation, and the law that the consuls applied in the exercise of their jurisdiction, lead to the conclusion that the Consulates of Valencia, Mallorca, Barcelona, and Perpignan were defined on their founding as strictly maritime institutions, and the Tortosa Consulate as a maritime-fluvial corporation.

The social basis for these five consulates, at the time of their first period as functioning organizations, consisted of navigators, including seamen and maritime merchants of the sea and maritime merchants, although the inclusion of merchants in these consulates must have been quite limited at first, which explains why, in the beginning, these consulates revolved, fundamentally, around seamen.

Regarding the competences, or legal powers, that the monarchy gave these consulates, the main objective pursued with their foundation was none other than the rapid resolution of conflicts that arose during commercial maritime navigation.

And with regard to the law applied by the consuls of the institutions in question, it should be noted that in the exercise of the jurisdiction received from the monarchy, these officials applied justice following maritime law and the theoretical and practical knowledge of maritime professionals, as can be seen in some of their founding documents, and in the rest of the surviving documentation.

However, this situation underwent a major and important change with the progressive inclusion of merchants (especially with that of some merchants with interests not only in maritime trade, but also in land) to the consulates of Valencia, Mallorca, Barcelona, Perpignan, and Tortosa, and to their governing bodies, with the consequent displacement of the seamen. This ended up causing these maritime consulates to be converted, in the late Middle Ages, into commercial consulates, thus taking on powers not only over maritime deals but also over land negotiations. This extension of jurisdiction to the oldest Aragonese maritime consulates took place through a succession of rules that span almost a century, the cycle opening in 1362 at the Consulate of Valencia, and closing there, too, in 1493.[18]

The Gerona consulate had both maritime and land competencies from its foundation in 1385, so it was a commercial consulate from the start. The same thing happened when the Consulate of Lleida was founded in 1510. The only Aragonese consulate which did not have jurisdiction over land trade issues seems to have been San Feliu de Guixols.

The significant arrival of the merchants in the Aragonese consulates inevitably led to some resistance from the seamen. However, the change took place, and the open support that the Aragonese monarchy gave to this transformation

---

18 See Serna Vallejo, 2018b: 318-319.

was decisive, granting the former maritime consulates the privilege of expanding their jurisdiction to land-based commercial acts, which meant relegating the seamen to the background from then on.

The Foundation of the Consulate of Burgos in the Context of the Disputes with Bilbao for the Control of Trade in the Northern Part of the Kingdom of Castile

Unlike the first Aragonese consulates, the Consulate of Burgos, like the vast majority of those founded later in Castilian lands, was designed, from the very moment of its foundation, as a commercial consulate, so that in the Kingdom of Castile there were no strictly maritime consulates as there had been in the Kingdom of Aragon during the first phase. The only exception is the Consulate of Seville which, from the start, was a maritime consulate with an indissoluble link to transoceanic trade.[19]

The fact that the initiative for the foundation of the first Castilian consulate came from the

---

19 Serna Vallejo, 2018b: 324-327.

merchant university of the city of Burgos, in the interior of Castile, at a point far from the coast, and the knowledge that the Catholic monarchs enacted the consolidation of the mercantile consulates in the Mediterranean area, explains how the Burgos consulate was of a commercial nature from the start. And that is why its competences concerned both maritime and land trade. In fact, some of the most consequential powers received by the institution related to maritime traffic as a result of Castilian trade with Flanders at the end of the fifteenth century, in which the merchants of Burgos played a leading role.

Based on two allusions made to the Consulates of Barcelona and Valencia in the regulations of July 21, 1494, issued by the Catholic monarchs to found the Consulate of Burgos, historiography—both domestic and international—has repeatedly highlighted the importance of those two Aragonese consulates in the definition of the consular institution in Castile at the dawn of the modern era.[20]

---

20 It is important to note that these references do not appear in the operative part of the norm, but in the part of the royal order in which the circumstances justifying the decision of the monarchy to create the Burgos consulate

Fortunately, however, this historiographic trend was interrupted by two works published in 1969[21] and 1979,[22] which notably qualified the weight that those two consulates had over that of Burgos and, ultimately, over the rest of the consulates in the Castilian area, including that of Bilbao.

Certainly, in view of the allusions to the Consulates of Barcelona and Valencia in the 1494 provision, it would be possible to consider in a first approximation that the Burgos consulate was founded with their structure and organization as a guideline. However, the comparative study of the three institutions allows us to conclude that the Catholic monarchs departed from the Aragonese model in some major ways, thus defining a new type of consulate. It is not unreasonable to state, therefore, that the Aragonese influence was not of significant weight in the composition, organization, and

---

are explained. It explains that the prior and consuls of the Burgos mercantile university had asked the monarchs to found the consulate in "the way the merchants of the cities of Barcelona and Valencia had." García de Quevedo, 1905: 153 and 155.

21 García Sanz, 1969.

22 Coronas González, 1979.

structure of the Consulate of Burgos. It was, however, significant in the decision to accept the creation of a consular institution in what was, at the time, the main commercial city in northern Castile, but whose hegemony was already being disputed by the town of Bilbao, just founded in 1300.

Hence, the creation of the Burgos consulate in 1494 was linked to the disagreements and confrontations that existed between the merchants of Burgos and Bilbao (many of whom were owners of ships) due to the pre-eminence of both in the field of commerce. This struggle led to both Burgos and Bilbao resorting to different tactics to gain control of trade, especially maritime trade, between the northern part of the Kingdom of Castile and European commercial cities, one of these strategies being the foundation of their respective consulates. Burgos considered that by having the first Castilian consulate it had placed itself ahead of Bilbao in the dispute for dominance over maritime trade. And the capital of Bizkaia was aware that it could not afford to lack an institution similar to that of Burgos if it wanted to keep up with that commercial city in the interior of Castile, or even surpass it.[23]

The initiative for the foundation of the Consulate of Burgos came from the university, or brotherhood of merchants, dedicated to the Holy Spirit, probably in the mid-fifteenth century and based on a previous institution from the eleventh century.[24] So, in the case of Burgos, and unlike what had happened in the Aragonese consulates, the impulse for its foundation did not come from the municipal government, although the Burgos merchants undoubtedly had its support—an understandable collaboration if one takes into account that some of the most notable merchants of the city were part of the local government of Burgos at different times.

As a consequence of this reality, it should be noted that in Burgos the consulate was never dependent on or subordinate to local government as consulates had been further east. So, the Consulate of Burgos was always

23 González Arce, 2009.

24 On the merchants' university of Burgos prior to the foundation of the consulate, see Basas Fernández, 1963: 32-33 and 49-51; García de Quevedo, 1905: 30-46; and González Arce, 2010.

linked directly to the monarchy and its officials in the town, mainly the *corregidor* (magistrate) and the *merino*.

On the other hand, and in direct relation to the subjects who had promoted the founding of the consulate, the human basis for the Burgos institution were merchants, and not seamen, who, on the contrary, had been the most important human element in the early days of the consulates of the Kingdom of Aragon.

It should also be noted that the Castilian consular institute had, from the first moment, a well-defined internal organization and its own rights as a consequence of having inherited or assumed the administrative structure and the ordinances of the old merchants' brotherhood of the Holy Spirit, an inheritance that had not happened, or at least not with the same intensity, in the consulates of the Mediterranean area (with the exception, perhaps, of the consulates of Barcelona and Tortosa, which had emerged from the recasting of two previous institutions). This explains why the Burgos consulate had, from the start, an assembly of confreres, a prior, two consuls, and several deputies,[25] as well as some ordinances (those of the previous institution). Notwithstanding, the rule of 1494 stated that after the constitution of the consulate, its leaders could draft new ordinances that would be presented to the Council of Castile for approval by the monarchy.

The last contrast between the Aragonese consulates and the Burgos consulate concerns the authority to resolve the appeals that could be filed against sentences handed down by consular courts in the first place. According to the norm of 1494, appeals against these sentences had to be resolved by the *corregidor* of the city, accompanied by two merchants—a formula very different from that implemented in the Aragonese institutions, in which, as a rule, the power to hear the appeals was held by the appeals judge of each consulate. At the same time, the Burgos merchants themselves had submitted a request to the monarchy that appeals be resolved by two merchants, as was the custom in Barcelona and Valencia, and that cases be resolved by them without any

---

25 González Arce, 2010: 165.

intervention by royal officials, which is what the monarchy finally decreed.

Bourbon Reformism and the Consular Institution in the Eighteenth Century

Bourbon reformism of the eighteenth century notably affected the consular institutions of the monarchy in two different ways, which does not prevent us from identifying some connections between the two. Firstly, some of the consulates inherited from previous centuries underwent profound remodelling, which in practice led to the definition of a new consular model. And secondly, the crown decided to create several consulates in different places, both in the Mediterranean and Atlantic areas, where institutions of this nature had never existed before, taking as a starting point the model that emerged from that reform, although at the same time other innovations were also incorporated. The first of the situations affected, among others, the consulates of Barcelona and Burgos, while the second led to the founding of several new consulates such as those in La

Coruña, Alicante, Santander, Malaga, Tenerife, Seville, and Valencia.[26]

Based on the above two situations and with a new approach that meant that the monarchy had to deal with the civil and political government of the nation, as well as with its economic government, the monarchy decided to intervene in the economic activity of the country using the consulates as a tool to that end. In the context of the economic reforms of the eighteenth century, the crown rejected the option of a single consulate above all others to deal exclusively with the promotion of the economy.[27] To the contrary, the crown positively viewed, from a governmental perspective, the convenience that all consulates—positioned on the same level, without any difference in category between them, contributing in equal measure to promoting the economic activity of

---

26 We include among the newly created the consulate of Seville because the old consulate established in Seville in 1543 moved to Cadiz in 1717, so Seville lost its consulate until a new one was founded in 1784; and the Valencia consulate because the institution of medieval origin stopped working around the year 1700, and in the second half of the eighteenth century a new consulate was founded there.

27 For information about the Madrid Consulate, see Serna Vallejo, 2018b: 327-332.

the nation—received competences in commercial matters and also in the fields of agriculture and other industries. This was a forecast that required the expansion of the social base of consular institutions to make entry possible for other groups besides merchants.

The most important consular renovation in the eighteenth century was the one that affected the Consulate of Barcelona in 1758,[28] and which led to the constitution of the three Commerce Corps of Catalonia. The importance of this change should be highlighted, among other reasons, because the new consular model ended up being extended, in one way or another and pretty much expressly, to most of the consulates in the rest of the country. However, the Consulate of Bilbao did not undergo that change.

---

28 In fact, the 1758 reform was not carried out on the Barcelona consulate of medieval origin, but on the Barcelona consulate established during the 1714–1716 biennium. This was because the Consulate of Barcelona, founded during the Middle Ages, had faded away after the entry of Felipe V's troops in Barcelona, and it was replaced by a new model consulate. On the new model Barcelona consulate and on the Commerce Corps of Catalonia, see Serna Vallejo, 2014: 744-763.

The consulate of 1758 was no longer the consulate of the city of Barcelona, as had been the case with the medieval consulate and the new model consulate that had previously existed in the city: it was, rather, the Consulate of the Principality of Catalonia. Furthermore, it was no longer an institution limited to maritime and land commercial exchanges: it had been founded as an economic institution in the broad sense, assuming powers in other areas of the economy beyond the strictly commercial.

The design of the latest generation of consulates (those established in the eighteenth century) was linked to the October 12, 1778 regulations for free trade from Spain to the Indies. In these regulations, which reformed the conditions of trade with the Indies, the monarchy gave authorization to several cities whose ports had been enabled for transoceanic trade (both in the peninsula and in the colonies) for the establishment of their respective consulates.[29]

And now, taking as a point of reference the evolution of the consular institution in the context of the monarchy, it is time to address

---

29 Serna Vallejo, 2018b: 341-342.

how plans for the Consulate of Bilbao began to take shape in 1495, although the final decree for its foundation was passed in 1511.

The Creation of the Consulate of Bilbao: A Process Started in 1495 and Concluded in 1511

Historiography about the origins of the Bilbao consulate has focused its attention preferentially, if not exclusively, on the year 1511, the date of the decree issued by Queen Joanna for its foundation. And although in some cases the royal decrees of 1495 that restricted the jurisdiction granted to the Consulate of Burgos in 1494 benefited the merchants of Bizkaia, Araba, and Gipuzkoa, we believe that the fundamental importance that these regulations had for the early foundation of the Consulate of Bilbao has not been sufficiently highlighted.

In 1495, the monarchy granted the university and merchant guild of the city of Bilbao most of the powers that a year before had been attributed exclusively to the Consulate of Burgos, although certainly the main function that allows the existence of a consulate, in the strict sense, had not yet been granted. In other words, the jurisdictional powers that would allow the new institution to judge on commercial cases, overcoming the narrow framework of guild jurisdiction that had previously been held by the Bilbao merchants' brotherhood and university, were finally granted in 1511.[30]

For these reasons, it does not seem excessive to state that although the final point of the foundation of the Consulate of Bilbao was in 1511, the path to its creation began in 1495, at the time when Bilbao merchants, with the support of others from Araba and Gipuzkoa, requested the monarchy grant various powers that it had already granted to the Consulate of Burgos the previous year, on its foundation.

The creation of the Consulate of Bilbao was carried out taking the Consulate of Burgos as a point of reference, as is clear from the privilege for its foundation, granted by Queen Joanna on

---

30 Prior to the establishment of the consulate, the Bilbao merchants' brotherhood and university only had jurisdiction over one guild, carried out by its senior officers, whose scope was limited to the knowledge of the minor cases that its members faced. The appeals against the sentences given in this first stage had to be brought before the council's regular jurisdiction, which in turn, was competent to decide on cases of greater substance that affected the members of the brotherhood and university of merchants.

June 22, 1511.[31] The document reproduces the founding text of the Burgos consulate of 1494 because it states that the Bilbao consulate was to be governed "by the aforementioned laws and its chapters" that a few years before had been given to the prior, consuls, and merchants of the city of Burgos.

The monarchy's decision to model the founding of the new Bilbao consulate after that of the first Castilian consulate, converged with the royal desire to also replicate the structure of that of Burgos—in the differences it had compared to the Aragonese consulates. The will of the merchants and captains of Bilbao ships to obtain their own consulate and be in the same position as the city of Burgos, in terms of commercial activity, was crucial in the decision for how to found the consulate. This claim must be placed in the context of the constant disagreement that Burgos and Bilbao had had for several decades about the control of commercial exchanges, despite the fact that, in reality, the merchants of both places needed each other. Burgos merchants needed Bilbao

---

31   The complete text of the Old Regime Laws of 1511 in *Prematicas, Ordenanças*, 1552.

ships to transport their merchandise, especially wool. The Bilbao shipmasters needed their vessels to be chartered by merchants from Burgos to their transport merchandise. And both Burgos and Bilbao needed insurance for commercial trips, arrangements for which were agreed on in Burgos because it was, at the time, the great center for contracting commercial insurance, especially maritime insurance, in the north of the Kingdom of Castile.

The confrontation between Burgos and Bilbao was recorded by many testimonies. One example is the Bilbao council's need to approve an ordinance in 1489 to set certain rules about the chartering of Bilbao ships for trips to some of the main European ports, such as those in Brittany and France, by merchants from different places, and from Burgos. The approval of this ordinance on August 14, 1489, by the town council of Bilbao, led to complaints from the people of Bilbao that the merchants of Burgos had prevented them from loading their merchandise, especially iron, on the ships that the people from Burgos had chartered in the port of Bilbao to be sent to those European trading cities. The norm decreed that when the people from Burgos or their hosts in Bilbao—their agents for transporting the goods by ship—chartered French or Breton vessels, they had to find out whether there were merchants interested in loading their merchandise onto the ships chartered by them, and the representative of the Bilbao merchants was given a period of three days to respond. If there were merchants willing to load their merchandise onto the ships hired by the people from Burgos, the latter were obliged to accept it on board the vessels.[32]

Inevitably, the disagreements between Burgos and Bilbao, far from dissipating, intensified after the foundation of the Burgos consulate in 1494. Nor did they disappear after the foundation of the Bilbao consulate at the beginning of the sixteenth century. This made it necessary for the merchants and institutions of both cities to adopt different measures, fundamentally terminating prior agreements, in order to try to preserve a certain degree

32 Ordinances of the Bilbao council from 1489–1490 published in Enríquez Fernández, Hidalgo de Cisneros Amestoy, Martínez Lahidalga, 1999b: 600-604.

of cordiality between the two commercially
rivalrous communities.

*The Reaction of Bilbao City Council and the
University and Brotherhood of Merchants
and Shipmasters on the Foundation of the
Consulate of Burgos*

The misgivings and resistance that the people
of Bilbao felt and showed for the creation of the
Burgos consulate explains how, immediately
after its foundation in 1494, they sent their
complaints to the monarchy,[33] in alliance
with the rest of Bizkaia, as well as Araba and
Gipuzkoa. Merchants in Bizkaia from towns
other than Bilbao, as well as those from Araba
and Gipuzkoa, supported the Bilbao position
and grouped together in their brotherhood and
university.[34] This union had some precedents

---

33 For the complaints presented to the monarchy by the
Bizkaians, see García de Quevedo, 1905: 163-164.

34 Although the religious brotherhood of Santiago had
existed from time immemorial, it seems that the mercantile
corporation, or university of merchants, that was linked to
it, and that was to lead to the foundation of the Consulate
of Bilbao, must have been set up in the second half of the
fifteenth century. For information about this brotherhood
and university, see Guiard y Larrauri, I, 1913: LXXXII,
5-7; García Fernández, 2005: 282-289; and González

in that on previous occasions merchants from the provinces of Araba and Gipuzkoa had allied with the people of Bizkaia in defense of their interests. That explains why the people of Gipuzkoa and Araba joined the Bizkaian merchants' corporation in Bruges, while the people from Bizkaia still had most of the power within the organization.[35] So, it can be said that the merchants and shipping companies of Bilbao were building an economic-commercial framework in which to bring together at least the people of Bizkaia, Araba, and Gipuzkoa.[36]

After the creation of the Burgos consulate, the complaints presented to the Catholic monarchs by the merchants from the three territories (Bizkaia, Araba, and Gipuzkoa) were directed fundamentally against the provisions contained in the 1494 norm regarding the foundation of consular jurisdiction, the organization of charters, the demands caused

---

Arce, 2019. And although this university, which was to give rise to the Consulate of Bilbao, brought together the captains and masters of ships as well as the merchants and traders, to simplify our description we will refer to it in an abbreviated way as the brotherhood and university of traders or merchants of Bilbao.

35 García Fernández, 2005: 285.

36 García Fernández, 2005: 288.

by tariffs and other rights,[37] the rendering of accounts by agents based in other trading cities (especially abroad), and for the drafting of commercial regulations. These complaints were linked, from the start, with a situation in which a consulate like that of Burgos could be founded with power over trade in Bizkaia, Araba, and Gipuzkoa and their areas of influence.

The granting of consular jurisdiction to the prior and consuls of Burgos—a privilege that meant that powers were given not only over its members, as had happened with the guild jurisdiction that had previously been exercised by the Brotherhood of the Holy Spirit, but also over all the Castilian merchants, both outside and within Castile, far exceeding the limited guild framework—inevitably displeased

37 In this context of taxation, the tariff was the rate required for goods transported by sea, a concept that should not be confused with general averages and particular averages, two legal factors with a long tradition in maritime law but with very different content. General averages allowed the distribution, among all those interested in shared maritime journeys, of the economic cost of the damages or expenses that any of them faced, deliberately saving a ship, its cargo, or both at the same time, from a known and actual risk. While particular averages, negatively defined, compared with general averages, were any damage or expense caused during a maritime voyage not considered to be general averages that had to be covered by the owner of the damaged asset.

the merchants and shipmasters of Bilbao who believed that the creation of this consular jurisdiction meant that Burgos had a preferential position in the framework of Castilian trade. This explains why immediately, in 1494 itself, they decided to petition the monarchy about the need to set up another consular organization in Bilbao similar to the Burgos one. They wanted equal conditions to those in the capital (at the time) of Castile, and for the Law of 1494 to not negatively affect the commercial activity of Bizkaia, Gipuzkoa, and Araba.

In terms of chartering, the 1494 provision gave the Burgos prior and consuls two far-reaching powers that, in practice, gave Burgos a freight monopoly. For one thing, it gave them the power to determine charter contracts for ships on which merchandise was to be loaded, both in the County and Lordship of Bizkaia and the Province of Gipuzkoa, and in "the Coastal Towns[38] and Merindad de Trasmiera" for trade with the main European ports. And, for another, it granted power to communicate (to

---

38 There were four towns in the Corregimiento de las Cuatro Villas de la Costa: San Vicente de la Barquera, Santander, Laredo, and Castro Urdiales.

all merchants in Burgos, in the cities of Segovia, Gasteiz, and Logroño, and towns of Valladolid and Medina de Rioseco, as well as any other town in which there was commercial activity) the contracting of such charters, as well as the dates on which the merchants would have to deliver their goods to be shipped, so that they could be made available to the masters of the ships within the deadlines set in the charter contracts drawn up by the authorities at the Burgos consulate.[39] At the same time, the norm gave priority for these charters to ships owned by subjects of the Catholic monarchs, over foreign-owned ships—although at that time that particular clause did not seem to be a cause of concern for the traders of Bilbao or their sphere of influence.

Resistance to such clauses was due to the fact that their content would prevent the Bilbao merchants' brotherhood and university from intervening in the chartering of ships

---

39 The Law of 1494 only refer to wool since it was, at that time, the main merchandise with which Burgos merchants traded, but inevitably this reference has to be interpreted in a broad sense as synonymous with any merchandise, including iron—which was going be so important for merchants linked to the Consulate of Bilbao.

for transporting goods to the main European ports, which, in the opinion of people from the lordship, violated the practice which had been followed until then and by which a consul from Burgos and another from Bizkaia oversaw chartering ships. That practice had allowed all fleets to ship merchandise from other nations in addition to from Castile, including that of some merchants from the Lordship of Bilbao and the Provinces of Araba and Gipuzkoa. Some charters, on the other hand, had always been carried out in the places on the coast where ships and merchandise were both to be found, and never in the interior, in the city of Burgos, as covered by the 1494 rule.

Regarding the agents that Castilian merchants had in the different trading cities, the Law of 1494 established, first, the obligation that, regardless of their place of residence, agents had the obligation to travel annually to Burgos to account for the merchandise and goods that the merchants had entrusted them with, and that they were subject to the Burgos consular jurisdiction for any debts they had taken on during these deals. Secondly, the

1494 laws prohibited them from demanding new tariffs or other rights on merchandise apart from those that they had traditionally demanded. Thirdly, they obligatorily linked expenditure of the amounts received for these tariffs to payment for things necessary and common to all merchants. And, finally, the laws established the duty of agents to send accounts for tariffs and rights received on the merchandise annually to the Burgos consular authorities, located in Medina del Campo, at the time of that town's fair. The objective of this forethought was to make it possible for such accounts to be reviewed by two merchants from Burgos and another two from cities outside of Castile who were at the fair. In addition, the Law of 1494 made this clause retroactive by requiring that the rendering of accounts for the previous six years also be carried out according to this procedure.

Furthermore, it was decided that once the accounts had been examined, the four merchants who had reviewed them could establish some new taxes on the merchandise in order to meet expenses which would be to the common good of all merchants. That clause concerned the people of Bizkaia because they understood that if merchants from the Lordship of Bizkaia and the Provinces of Araba and Gipuzkoa did not take part in the establishment of those tariffs or rights, then people from Burgos could set heavy, excessive rights for their own interests.

And, finally, the last clause in the Law of 1494, which the people of Bizkaia opposed, referred to the power granted to the Consulate of Burgos to draft general ordinances that would bind not only its associates but also all Castilian merchants once they received royal approval. Bizkaian reluctance was due to the same fear as in the previous case. The concern was that the ordinances that could be drawn up unilaterally by the Burgos consulate to benefit its own associates and harm the merchants of the Lordship of Bizkaia and the Provinces of Araba and Gipuzkoa.

The Response of the Monarchy to the Claims of Bizkaia, Gipuzkoa, and Araba

The protests and proposals made to the Castilian monarchy by the people of Bizkaia, Gipuzkoa, and Araba had immediate positive effects, making the monarchy see the convenience of specifying the scope of the 1494 rule in order to improve the situation of the claimants, a clarification that, in fact, was largely a rectification that was specified in three clauses dated February 14, September 20, and November 12, 1495.[40]

The relevance and transcendence of these norms are of great importance; surprisingly, however, historiography has not recognized them as such. Note that with the new features in these measures, the jurisdiction initially granted to the Burgos consulate in 1494 was considerably reduced, favoring the commercial interests of those who had their commercial operations centers in Bilbao and its surroundings, while they served to initiate the process for the foundation of the Consulate of Bilbao, which was to take place in 1511.

---

40 The clause dated November 12, 1495, while not mentioned by other sources, is mentioned in García de Quevedo, 1905: 52.

The claim presented against the foundation of the Consulate of Burgos was dealt with by the Council of Castile between the end of 1494 and the beginning of 1495, on a date that we currently cannot specify with absolute precision but that allowed the monarchy to provide an initial response to the petitioners on February 14, 1495.[41] With this provision, the monarchy excluded merchants from the Lordship of Bizkaia and the Provinces of Araba and Gipuzkoa from Burgos consular jurisdiction with a single exception. The commercial lawsuits that might have been brought previously, or that were to be brought from this point on, between the merchants of these three territories and the merchants of the city of Burgos, or their consorts, agents, and servants, would continue to be the responsibility of the Consulate of Burgos. All the other lawsuits—which, consequently, did not concern the people from Burgos—could continue to be brought and judged before the ordinary courts if they exceeded the strict guild framework of the Bilbao merchants' brotherhood and university.

---

41 For the text of the response of February 14, 1495, see García de Quevedo, 1905: 164-166.

As for the distribution of tariffs and other rights regarding merchandise, the people of Burgos were prohibited from making decisions that would place people from the Lordship of Bizkaia and the Provinces of Araba and Gipuzkoa under obligation, and reciprocally it was determined that those from Bizkaia, Araba, and Gipuzkoa could not agree on tariffs or other rights that prejudiced Burgos' interests. And, with the aim of being able to cover shared expenses for all merchants, both from Burgos and the Lordship of Bizkaia and the Provinces of Araba and Gipuzkoa, the idea that some representatives from both areas would meet to set the scope of distributions that would affect everyone equally was taken into consideration.

Regarding the accounts of the agents that the merchants of the Lordship of Bizkaia and the Provinces of Araba and Gipuzkoa had in the different trading cities, mainly around Europe, some new features were also introduced. It was established that the accounts would be sent to the representatives of these merchants, who would present them annually at the Medina del Campo fair, where they would have to be reviewed by six merchants—specifically, by three from the Lordship and the Provinces and by three from Burgos and other cities and towns in the Kingdom of Castile who traded outside the kingdom and were at the fair. The same procedure was applied retroactively for the accounts of the previous six years.

And, finally, in response to objections raised in terms of the provisions of the Law of 1494 regarding chartering (the clause that had caused the greatest concern in Bilbao), the Catholic monarchs decided to delegate to the Consulate of Burgos and to the merchants of the Lordship of Bizkaia and the Provinces of Araba and Gipuzkoa the drawing up of a procedure that could be implemented with the approval of both parties, demanding that the interested parties themselves agree on the procedure. To that end, it was ordered that "before Lent in the year ninety-five" six merchants from each of the parties should meet in the Burgos province town of Briviesca, an intermediate point between Bilbao and Burgos, and that they should agree upon the best way to carry out the charters and should outline this in some ordinances that would have to be sent to the Council of Castile to seek royal approval.

At the same time, the Catholic monarchs, aware of the difficulties that would undoubtedly arise in Burgos and Bilbao trying to reach an agreement of this nature, foresaw, in the event of the Briviesca meeting failing, that each of the parties would send two representatives to the Council of Castile with information about all the negotiations that had taken place during the unsuccessful meeting so that, finally, the council could agree on a decision.

At this point, and in view of the contents of the February 1495 measure, it should be underlined that more than a clarification of the clauses of the 1494 law, it was in fact a rectification by the monarchy that entailed the withdrawal from the Consulate of Burgos of some of the powers that had been granted to it in 1494 and their reassignment to the university and merchant guild of Bilbao. And this means that although a consulate was not founded in Bilbao at that time, since consular jurisdiction was not granted to the citizens of Bilbao, some of the foundations that a few years later would facilitate its creation were laid. It should also be noted that while this reallocation of powers between the two institutions was carried out, ways of collaboration were set between them to resolve some issues, as if it had been thought that it was possible to satisfy the merchants of Burgos and Bilbao and establish channels of dialogue between them in order to settle conflict and avoid the foundation, at least for the moment, of a second consulate.

The Unsuccessful Meeting at Briviesca and the New Royal Decision of September 20, 1495

In compliance with the February 1495 decree from the Catholic monarchs regarding chartering, the representatives of the Consulate of Burgos and the Lordship of Bizkaia and the Provinces of Araba and Gipuzkoa met in the town of Briviesca to try to agree on the regime under which the charters that merchants affected from these territories should be organized from then on. However, as the Catholic monarchs themselves feared, the discussions did not bear the desired fruit, and for that reason two merchants from each of the parties had to appear before the Council of Castile. And once their allegations had been heard, the monarchs announced the cancellation of the monopoly for the charter of ships that the Law of 1494 had established to the benefit of the Consulate of Burgos and its associates.

In this new royal decision, dated September 20, 1495,[42] and which was officially certified in January 1496 at the request of the Burgos Consulate,[43] it was decreed that the merchants of Burgos, of the Lordship of Bizkaia, of the Provinces of Araba and Gipuzkoa, or of any other place, could charter ships with total autonomy, and that the merchants could load their merchandise in any of the ships that were part of fleets bound for European ports, regardless of who chartered them. So, a solution was sought that, at least for the moment, could reassure the people of Bilbao on the issue of chartering, which was the one that most concerned them.

---

42 For the text of the decision of September 20, 1495, see García de Quevedo, 1905: 167-169

43 In García de Quevedo, 1905: 169-170.

In terms of tariffs, the situation of merchants linked to the Lordship of Bilbao and the Provinces of Araba and Gipuzkoa was also improved by establishing that the Consulate of Burgos and the Bilbao merchants' brotherhood and university could only set new tariffs and rights that compelled the associates of both parties when their purpose was to favor the common good of all merchants.

The Agreement of December 7, 1499, between the Consulate of Burgos and the Council of Bilbao

The corrections made by the monarchy in 1495 to the Law of 1494 were not, however, sufficient to appease the disagreements between the Consulate of Burgos and the merchants of Bilbao,[44] and so, over the following years, the disagreements between Burgos and Bilbao continued to take place, harming the merchants of both parties. And it is precisely in this context that the signing of an agreement on December

---

44 On the conflictive relationship between the Consulate of Burgos and the merchants and the Council of Bilbao, see González Arce, 2009.

7, 1499, between the Consulate of Burgos and the Council of Bilbao took place, aiming to put an end to the conflict between the merchants of both towns.[45]

This agreement is important because it allowed Bilbao merchants to continue to improve their situation with regard to Burgos with the express recognition of the Burgos consular authorities, implicitly softening some of the circumstances in which Burgos could oppose the creation of a consulate in the capital of Bizkaia.

The Capitulation of 1499

The concord of 1499 was negotiated between the prior and consuls of the university of merchants of Burgos and Pedro López de Vitoria,[46] who had received powers from the Bilbao merchants for that purpose.[47] Pedro López de Vitoria was

---

45 The text of the agreement signed in December 1499 can be seen in Guiard y Larrauri, I, 1913: 16-19 and also in Enríquez Fernández, Hidalgo de Cisneros Amestoy, Martínez Lahidalga, 2000: 1191-1195.

46 Enríquez Fernández, Hidalgo de Cisneros Amestoy, Martínez Lahidalga, 2000: 1188-1189.

47 The organization of the municipal government of Bilbao

a merchant and the master of a ship, who lived in Bilbao, although he was from Gasteiz, and who, in the 1480s and 1490s, held various positions in the local government of Bilbao: mayor (1483), *regidor* (1487), and *fiel de la villa* (town councillor) (1488, 1492, 1495, and 1499).[48]

The sixteen chapters of the concord included different agreements with respect to freight, the loading of merchandise, tariffs, and the geographical space which the jurisdiction of the Consulate of Burgos and the university and brotherhood of Bilbao covered.

The first chapter envisaged the annual organization of a single fleet bound for Flanders in order to avoid the dangers and damages that many vessels had to face while sailing alone.

---

was modified in 1435 in an agreement signed between the town council and the major noble families there. At that time, among other issues, a new order was established for the elections of council positions and the existence of a single mayor. Furthermore, the text registered the existence of the merchants' representatives, who were not the same as the council's representatives. See the ratification (passed by John II) of the anti-bandit ordinances and regulations proposed by the town of Bilbao (June 10, 1435). Enríquez Fernández, Hidalgo de Cisneros Amestoy, Martínez Lahidalga, 1999a: 248-270.

48 Salazar Arechalde, 2003: 196.

The responsibility for the formation of this fleet had to be shared, alternating between either the prior and consuls of the Consulate of Burgos or the representative of the merchants of Bilbao, and it depended on the nature of the cargo that was to be transported on the ships. For wool and other goods that were not iron or steel, the chartering of the vessels was to be managed by the Burgos authorities, which could charter the ships for this negotiation both in the Bilbao canal and at any other point on the coast. Whereas if it were a question of hiring ships to transport iron and steel, the organization of the chartering of the vessels was to be done by the representative of the merchants of Bilbao. It was also decided that the merchants of Bilbao and Burgos could load a percentage of their merchandise—up to a third of the capacity of the vessels in the ships hired by the other party—for the same prices that the charterers demanded from the merchants of their own organization.

In the second chapter, the same measure was applied to the chartering of ships and the loading of goods bound for Brittany, especially in Nantes and La Rochelle. And the eighth chapter determined the penalty to be imposed on those who, in breach of the clauses of the first two precepts, chartered vessels for Flanders, Brittany, and La Rochelle on their own.

The third chapter of the concord was of special interest because it determined the geographical space over which the jurisdiction of the Consulate of Burgos and that of the university and merchant guild of Bilbao had to be extended in order to be able to demand from the merchants the amounts of the tariffs set by each institution, and to be able to take advantage of both entities' privileges. Furthermore, it was forbidden for either institution to take in merchants from the area belonging to the other institution.

The Burgos jurisdiction extended over the coastal towns of the Corregimiento de las Cuatro Villas de la Costa—San Vicente de la Barquera, Santander, Laredo, and Castro Urdiales—and over the inland towns of Logroño, Nájera, Medina de Pomar, Segovia, Valladolid, and Medina de Rioseco. While the Bilbao jurisdiction included the County of Bizkaia, Gipuzkoa, Araba, Gasteiz, and Encartaciones.

To ensure as much compliance as possible with the clauses of this chapter, in the next chapter, the fourth, both institutions were prohibited from loading merchandise from merchants who had breached the terms of the concord in ships chartered by their associates; the vessels of the non-compliant masters could not be chartered; and deals could not be made with anyone who disregarded the provisions of the agreement. At the same time, admitting into either of the two institutions people who did not comply with what was agreed to in the capitulation was prohibited.

The purpose of the fifth chapter was to guarantee the correct placement of goods on board ships, prohibiting stowage using "*draos*"[49] and demanding that lighter pieces of wood be used. The loss of the amount of the freight is stated as a sanction for those who failed to comply with the provisions of the regulation.

---

49 *Draos* were large pieces of heavy wood that were put in position and pulled by ropes, serving as mallets to apply great pressure on objects and move them. *Diccionario marítimo español*: 228.

The sixth, seventh, eleventh, and twelfth chapters referred to tariffs, their calculation dependent on the load of certain merchandise or goods (including arms and gunpowder for the defense of vessels under attack) and the destination.

The ninth chapter set some rules for the sale of merchandise, especially wool, in the warehouses that merchants had in Flanders.

And if the need arose to send a representative of the signatory institutions of the concord to court to raise any matter before the monarchy, the tenth chapter established that both the Consulate of Burgos and the Bilbao brotherhood could choose one or two people "together and in agreement" with the monarch to remedy whatever needed to be dealt with.

The thirteenth chapter was intended to guarantee financial aid for the churches of Santiago and San Anton in Bilbao and other pious works.

For the effective control of the charters carried out in Bilbao, the fourteenth chapter dealt with the notaries before whom the contracts were finalized and the custody of the chest in which such contracts should be kept. It was established that this responsibility was held by two notaries in the city of Bilbao, one designated by the prior and consuls of Burgos, and the other by the merchants of Bilbao.

And since the preservation of merchandise in Bilbao's fish markets was a concern for merchants because of the river flooding them with some frequency, the fifteenth chapter established the obligation for non-local merchants to have appropriate markets for the deposit and safe-keeping of the merchandise in order to avoid the damages that the flooding of the Nerbioi River could cause.

The Reform of the Concord on January 28, 1500

Some of the contents approved in 1499 were not to the liking of the Bilbao merchants who understood that certain chapters were harmful to their interests, which led to a first modification of the concord in 1500. Furthermore, several years later, in 1513, and therefore after the founding of the Consulate of Bilbao, an event took place that significantly altered the background of the relations between the merchants of Burgos and Bilbao, making it necessary to introduce more changes to the chapters of the concord. For now, we will address the 1500 reform. Later we will examine the 1513 reform.

On both occasions the initiative for the correction of the text started in Bizkaia, being the council and merchants of Bilbao who went to the Burgos consulate in order to incorporate some changes into the document, which inevitably required new negotiations between the parties.

In general terms, the interests of the Bilbao council and its merchants—first in the brotherhood of merchants of the University of Santiago in Bilbao, and later in the consulate— were the same, which allowed them to act together in the defense of the commercial interests of both the merchants and the town.[50] The fact that several of the major Bilbao merchants held positions of responsibility in the municipal government of the town must have contributed positively to this partnership.

---

50 García Fernández, 2005: 283.

However, in some situations the positions of the council and the merchants diverged, leading to some dissension between the two institutions. And this is precisely what happened after the signing of the concord in 1499 by the Consulate of Burgos and the Council of Bilbao, when the Bilbao merchants understood that all their needs had not been considered.

At the beginning of 1500, the Council of Bilbao granted powers to Flores González de Arteaga, Ochoa Sánchez de Larriniga, and Fernán Sánchez de las Ribas to begin the new negotiations that were to be held with the Burgos prior and consuls,[51] and again to Pedro López de Vitoria, the negotiator in 1499.[52] While the brotherhood and university of merchants of Bilbao gave powers to Ochoa Pérez de Uriondo.[53]

---

51 Although Sánchez de las Ribas is recorded to have had powers from the council, we believe that to be an error, and that he took part at the proposal of the university and the brotherhood.

52 Enríquez Fernández, Hidalgo de Cisneros Amestoy, Martínez Lahidalga, 2000: 1198-1200.

53 Enríquez Fernández, Hidalgo de Cisneros Amestoy, Martínez Lahidalga, 2000: 1200-1202.

As a result of the newly opened debate about the content of the concord, the meaning of its chapters was clarified in the following ways.[54]

To facilitate compliance with the provisions of the first chapter of the concord, the obligation was established for Burgos merchants to notify the representative of Bilbao merchants of their willingness to charter ships for the Flemish fleet fifteen to twenty days in advance of the date of the start of navigation, and for the people of Bilbao to inform the people of Burgos of the iron and steel that they intended to load onto the ships chartered by the people of Burgos, the maximum load quota being one third of the capacity of the vessels.[55]

The change in the second chapter allowed the merchants of Bilbao to charter vessels of smaller dimensions (of fifty or sixty barrels) to transport various merchandise without Burgos being able to ship any merchandise in such vessels. And in the eighth chapter it was

---

54 The text of these first reforms in Enríquez Fernández, Hidalgo de Cisneros Amestoy, Martínez Lahidalga, 2000: 1202-1206.

55 In the document there is a serious misprint: the merchants from Burgos being confused with those of Bilbao.

pointed out that the sanctions foreseen in the concord of 1499 were also applicable to this newly established situation.

In the fourth chapter, it was added that Burgos and Bilbao should together punish those who failed to comply with the clauses of the chapters, while providing for the fixing of some tariffs to cover common costs, dividing them equally between the two institutions.

As regards the question of the sale of merchandise foreseen in the ninth chapter, the clarification of 1500 was designed to fix Monday, Wednesday, and Friday (according to the custom that existed in Flanders, Nantes, and La Rochelle) for that purpose, while it was determined that the consuls of both parties were the ones who would set sanctions for noncompliance.

The purpose of the clarification of the tenth chapter was to establish the distribution of the expenses involved in sending commissioners or agents to the court (to raise any matter in connection with merchants before the monarchy) in a ratio of two to one between the Consulate of Burgos and the university and brotherhood of Bilbao. At the same time, it was determined that the amount of the fines that were imposed on the offenders would be used to defray the expenses incurred by the two institutions.

In the eleventh chapter, it was added that the calculation of tariffs included certain amounts in maravedis to pay notaries and clerks, as well as for the purchase of paper, ink, and other expenses. As regards the twelfth chapter, regarding the collection of tariffs, it was proposed that, at the expense of the Council of Bilbao, a house be built, within a year, to be called the "House for counting tariffs," where that task would be carried out for both outbound and return trips. Additionally, the people before whom the calculation was carried out would be recorded with precision in the tariff register, and members of the Consulate of Burgos and the merchants of Bilbao had to be present.

Regarding financial aid for the churches of Santiago and San Anton in Bilbao, and other pious works dealt with in the thirteenth chapter of the concord, the amount to be delivered for each sack of wool, quintal of iron, or other merchandises was specified.

In the fifteenth chapter, in which the merchants from Burgos were obliged to have appropriate markets for the deposit and safekeeping of their merchandise in Bilbao, the provision was added that the Council of Bilbao would take guarantees from the non-local merchants to be able to face damages that could happen due to river flooding.

Finally, two new chapters were added. The first included the clause that the chapters from 1499, with the corrections and additions of 1500, be applied for a period of twenty-five years from December 7, 1499. And, in the second, a new system was set forth for the payment of tariffs by foreigners to satisfy the consulates of Castile and Bizkaia in Flanders.

Once the reform of the chapters was agreed to at the end of January, 1500, it was necessary for the text to be presented to the council, councillors, and deputies of the town of Bilbao for approval, a requirement that was met on February 3 of that year.[56]

Queen Joanna Deals with the Claim of the Merchants of Bilbao and Establishes the Consulate in the Capital of Bizkaia

On the basis of the precedent of the Consulate of Burgos, of the powers granted to the brotherhood and university of Bilbao merchants in 1495 which involved a reduction of those initially granted in 1494 to the Burgos institution, and of the powers established in the concord agreed upon between the Council of Bilbao and the Burgos consulate in 1499 (reformed in 1500), finally the shippers, masters of ships, and merchants of Bilbao—a considerably broader group and, above all, more heterogeneous than the one that had promoted the founding of the Consulate of Burgos—decided to make a request to the monarchy to found a consulate in Bilbao.

In order to carry out this initiative, its promoters had the support of the council

---

56   In Enríquez Fernández, Hidalgo de Cisneros Amestoy, Martínez Lahidalga, 2000: 1206-1208.

authorities; however, this did not result in the establishment of an organic unit of the new consulate with respect to the Council of Bilbao. So, the Bizkaian consulate, like the Burgos consulate, and unlike the Aragonese ones, established itself as organically separate from the municipal government of the town, being immediately and directly subject to the monarchy.

Juan de Ariz was one of the most important merchants in the town of Bilbao since the late fifteenth century.[57] On behalf of the councillors and deputies of the brotherhood and university of "captains and masters of ships and merchants and traders" of the town of Bilbao, he was in charge of addressing the Council of Castile to request the creation of the consulate. In his presentation, he highlighted the similarities that existed between the councillors and the deputies of Bilbao university and the governing positions of the Burgos consulate; he drew attention to the existence of old ordinances of the Bilbao university, which had been confirmed by the monarchy; he recalled that the institution

---

57 Guiard y Larrauri, I, 1913: XCII.

had servants and agents in the major ports of Flanders, England, Britain, and elsewhere; and he finished by requesting that the university and brotherhood of Bilbao receive "the same form and order" that the Burgos consulate had.

The request was attended by Queen Joanna who, through a law passed in Seville on June 22, 1511, set up the Consulate of Bilbao and ordered that the new institution be governed by the provisions of the Old Regime Laws of 1494 that had enabled the foundation of the Consulate of Burgos.

In reality, and taking into account all the above, the real novelty that the 1511 provision entailed was the granting of two fundamental powers to the Bilbao merchants' brotherhood and university because, it should be remembered, the rest of the powers granted in 1494 to the people of Burgos had already been obtained by the people of Bilbao in 1495. The two new and fundamental powers received in 1511 were, on the one hand, consular jurisdiction—in other words, the creation of the consular court—and, on the other, the power to draw up ordinances. Thus, from that moment on, the old merchants' brotherhood and university, now transformed into a consulate, could understand factors that affected the merchandise. In other words, it could administer justice on commercial matters in the same way that all the other consulates of the monarchy did, and it was able to draw up its own ordinances for the government of the institution and bring order to commerce.

In this way, the Law of 1511 concluded the process that had begun in 1495 with the aim of ensuring that Bilbao had a consulate similar to that of Burgos: a mercantile consulate, with powers over both land and maritime trade, autonomous from the town government, and with a very broad social base that included merchants in the strict sense and the masters of ships and other navigators.

The Reform of the Concord in 1513

The 1500 update of the 1499 concord between the Consulate of Burgos and the Council of Bilbao enabled mercantile contract between people from Burgos and Bilbao to be regulated by its clauses for a time.[58] However, the situation changed when Burgos merchants began to use ports other than Bilbao to transport their goods, which led to new conflicts between the Consulate of Burgos and the recently founded Consulate of Bilbao.

In 1513, the attitude of the Burgos prior, consuls, and merchants forced the Bilbao council and the authorities of the Bilbao consulate to address the Burgos institution to seek a solution and request a new clarification of the old concord.[59]

Among the corrections incorporated on this date there was a clause for the fleets to Flanders to consist of seven ships; it was specified that the merchants of the town of Castrojeriz were to be included in the jurisdiction of the Consulate of Burgos; it was agreed that the days for the sale of merchandise in Flanders would be Monday, Wednesday, and Friday, and that in Nantes they would be Tuesday, Thursday, and Saturday; and the concord, which was being reformed

58 In Enríquez Fernández, Hidalgo de Cisneros Amestoy, Martínez Lahidalga, 2000: 1208-1209.

59 Enríquez Fernández, Hidalgo de Cisneros Amestoy, Martínez Lahidalga, 2000: 1209-1211.

once again, was to be valid for twenty years from the date it received royal confirmation.

Furthermore, some new chapters had to be added as a result of the changes that had taken place since 1511, at the same time as the foundation of the Consulate of Bilbao.

The first additional chapter was intended to resolve the open debate between the two consulates over the name that was used to appoint the officials of the new Bizkaian consulate. The terms that had been used since ancient times in the university and merchants' guild of Bilbao to name its most important officials had been *fiel* (representatives—literally, "faithful ones") and deputies, but since the foundation of the consulate, the highest representatives of the new consular institution came to be called priors and consuls because the Law of 1511 stipulated that the Bilbao consulate be founded in accordance with the guidelines given in the 1494 law which had founded the Consulate of Burgos and because the institution that was founded in Bilbao was, of course, a consulate.

In this context, from Burgos' point of view, any use of the terms "prior" and "consul" for the Consulate of Bilbao were viewed with suspicion, considering that the use of such terms should be restricted to the Burgos area, which they used to justify their opposition to and confrontation with the Bilbao institution and which was eventually taken to court. To resolve this disagreement, taking advantage of the reform of the concord in 1513, it was stipulated that, from that moment, the authorities of the Bilbao consulate could only call themselves *fiel* and deputies, while urging the monarchy to support this stipulation in the lawsuit that Burgos and Bilbao had pending on this issue before royal jurisdiction. Furthermore, the people of Bilbao undertook accepting the clauses of various judgments that had been handed down to resolve some of the disagreements that had arisen in Flanders between the consulates of the nations of Castile and Bizkaia.

It was also agreed that from now on the Burgos consular authorities, in their dealings of any kind, would give preference to the town of Bilbao and to the merchants' representatives and deputies, thus establishing an alliance between both towns and consulates.

The concord was ratified by the two consulates on June 13, 1513,[60] and it was presented to the Council of Castile for immediate confirmation, which took place on September 16 of the same year.[61]

The agreement of this new reform of the old concord of 1499 once again brought some tranquility to the relations between the consulates of Burgos and Bilbao, but in the end the disagreements between the two institutions appeared once more, so it became necessary to agree to new concords during the next two centuries.

---

60 Enríquez Fernández, Hidalgo de Cisneros Amestoy, Martínez Lahidalga, 2000: 1212-1220.

61 Enríquez Fernández, Hidalgo de Cisneros Amestoy, Martínez Lahidalga, 2000: 1220-1222.

The *Ius Proprium* Established by the Consulate of Bilbao: Decrees, Particular and General Ordinances, and, above all, the Ordinances of 1737

Prior to the establishment of the consulate, the old brotherhood and university of "captains and masters of ships and merchants and traders" of Bilbao had been governed by different rules dictated by the town council (because the regulation of maritime commercial traffic was controlled by the council), although the council authorities took into account the opinion and needs of the merchants in trading cities. And it is precisely these clauses, originally written by the Council of Bilbao, that some authors describe as the "first ordinances" of the Consulate of Bilbao.[62] However, given that these clauses were not norms established by the university and merchants' brotherhood, the immediate antecedent to the consulate, but rather authored by the town council, they could not be considered ordinances from the commercial institution (even though their contents still had to be

---

62 Blanco Constans, 1895: I, 229; Olaran Múgica, 2011.

fulfilled and complied with by the members of the commercial corporation that preceded the consulate, in the same way that all local government norms had to be observed by the citizens of Bilbao).[63] The spread of the idea that the Bilbao brotherhood and university had its own ordinances—at least according to parts of the historiography—may have been decisively influenced by the fact that the Law of 1511 stipulated the existence of ordinances for the institution among the arguments that the people of Bilbao made before the monarchy when requesting the foundation of the consulate.

Among those "primitive ordinances" drawn up by the Bilbao council authorities to order different facets of the town's commercial activity prior to the foundation of the consulate, it is worth mentioning, among others, those dated 1399, 1447, 1459 (a questionable date, as we will see shortly), 1489–1490, and 1509.[64]

---

63 Zabala y Allende, 1907: 46; Petit, 2016: 146.

64 Miren Edurne Gumuzio Añibarro's thesis, directed by María Jesús Cava Mesa and Santiago Larrazabal Basañez, defended at the University of Deusto in 2017, refers to these ordinances, as well as the consular ordinances themselves.

The ordinances of 1399 dealt with the trade in foreign wines.[65] Those of 1477 stipulated the obligation to declare the goods that were loaded and unloaded in the Bilbao canal.[66] And those of specifically August 11, 1447, whose existence is known due to a judgement made on April 2, 1563,[67] dealt with the measures of the cloth imported from France, England, Flanders, and the Duchy of Brittany, and the right for preferential acquisition for the residents of Bilbao. With regard to these 1447 ordinances, it must be taken into account that, from the information included in the testimony that we have of their existence, it seems clear that the town council issued them for the brotherhood of the Santa Cruz drapers, so that although their contents could affect and interest the members of the Bilbao merchants' guild and university, they were not specifically designed for that organization.[68]

---

65 Guiard y Larrauri, I, 1913: LXXXIII.

66 Guiard y Larrauri, I, 1913: LXXXIII-LXXXIV.

67 Zabala y Allende, 1907: 45-46.

68 The testimony from 1511 about the chapters of these ordinances, included in a judgement from 1563, is published in Enríquez Fernández, Hidalgo de Cisneros Amestoy, Martínez Lahidalga, 2000: 1110-1112.

Regarding the ordinances of 1459 mentioned by some authors, it should be noted that there are many doubts about their existence as there is no reliable testimony about their chapters and only certain mentions are made of them by some authors.[69] And it is precisely these uncertainties regarding their existence that raise the possibility that the date of these ordinances is an error and that, in fact, they are actually those dated 1489 and 1490.[70]

The ordinances of 1489 1490 are actually several individual chapters of a single ordinance, approved on different dates in these two years, and which, in March 1490, were collected together at the request of the representative of the merchants of the town.[71] They deal with, among other issues, the chartering of Bilbao ships for trips to the main European ports, such as those in Brittany and France, arranged

---

In the document there is evidence that the administrator of the Santa Cruz brotherhood of drapers asked the mayor of Bilbao for a legal copy of the chapters of the ordinance of his brotherhood from August 11, 1447.

69 Benito y Endara, 1896: 189.

70 Zabala y Allende, 1907: 44-45; Petit, 2016: 146.

71 In Enríquez Fernández, Hidalgo de Cisneros Amestoy, Martínez Lahidalga, 1999b: 600-601.

by merchants from different places (especially from Burgos) and the prohibition of loading in the canal without having taken *money of God* from the merchants' representative.[72]

And even in 1509, just two years before the Consulate of Bilbao was officially founded, it seems that the Bilbao council issued an ordinance for the common good of the town's university of merchants and ship masters.[73]

The Consulate's Own Rights between 1511 and 1737: Decrees, Agreements, and Particular and General Ordinances

From 1511 onward, after the foundation of the consulate, and although the validity of the ordinances issued by the Bilbao council were not modified in any way, the situation changed significantly because the new consulate, in addition to achieving legal powers, was also granted *potestas statuendi*—in other words,

---

72 *Money of God* was the symbolic exchange of a coin of little value that the merchants' representative gave to the masters of the ships to symbolize the granting of the license to begin loading the ships. González Arce, 2019: 202.

73 González Arce, 2019: 191.

the power for its governing bodies to draw
up ordinances and to adopt resolutions and
decrees. Thus, by making use of this power,
the consulate became the creator of its own
laws. Because these laws were prepared for the
benefit of those who were engaged in commercial
activity within the framework of the Bilbao
consulate, they should be viewed as privilege
laws (in addition to private and corporate).

In the first months of the consulate's
operation, it was governed by rules inherited,
to a large degree, from the previous stage (when
the organization had only been a university
and brotherhood), as specified in the text of
the general ordinances of 1531. However, very
soon its leaders saw the convenience of drafting
the clauses to regulate the internal working of
the institution, as well as different matters of
vital importance for trade by Bilbao shippers,
so both agreements and decrees issued by the
governing bodies of the institution—such as
ordinances—began to be set down in writing.
This initiative tried to guarantee the preservation
of the institution's own law, avoiding dangers
implicit in the oral transmission of customary

law, because that which is held and kept by unwritten custom is often lost and interpreted in different ways.[74]

The most solemn issues—those of greatest importance for the consulate—were discussed and dealt with by the majority of the consulate members in a general assembly. In these deliberations both those who held consular office and those who were part of the corporation without holding office, participated. Ordinary, everyday matters, on the other hand, were usually resolved by those who were in charge of the institution.

The decisions that were adopted in either of these two ways were specified in agreements or decrees, which were mandatory for all members of the consulate; these were provisions limited in length since they only included the strict agreements made. However, together with these agreements or decrees, the Consulate of Bilbao also began to pass ordinances, which, drafted and approved within the framework of the consulate, had to be sent to the Council of Castile, for confirmation by the monarchy,

---

74 In Guiard y Larrauri, I, 1913: 582-598, quotation, p. 583.

which was the established use in relation to all kinds of ordinances (including councils and guilds) in the Castilian sphere of influence.

As was generally the case in relation to the ordinances of all types of organizations, those of the Bilbao consulate were not all the same, so it is necessary to differentiate between particular ordinances and general ordinances. Beyond this differentiation, all the ordinances were drawn up with the intention of their having indefinite validity, enduring over time, and not needing to ever be reformed or replaced by a new chapter.

The particular, or sectoral, ordinances of the Consulate of Bilbao were intended to define the legal system for some particular matters, which is why they had a markedly casuistic nature, and are very diverse in what they undertake, as can be seen from a simple review of the contents of some of the ordinances of this category approved by the Consulate of Bilbao in the sixteenth and seventeenth centuries. Among the matters regulated in these particular ordinances, it is worth mentioning the choices about those who should carry out the offices of the corporation

(1512[75] and 1675[76]); the amounts to be paid for the average rights on the entry and exit of goods from the port (1517);[77] insurance contracts (1520[78] and 1558[79]); the pilot or coastal pilots who, in the case of Bilbao, were responsible for guiding ships when entering and leaving the port and the estuary (1561[80] and 1596[81]); the carrying out of sentences handed down by the consuls of the institution, and in which the favorable vote of two of the three judges concurred, both in the first and second instance (1597);[82] and the disputing or payment of bills (1672).[83] In addition, in 1687 five chapters of

75 In Guiard y Larrauri, I, 1913: 214-216.

76 Zabala y Allende, 1907: 50-51.

77 Ordinances of April 1517, confirmed by the monarchy in 1518, on tariffs. In Guiard y Larrauri, I, 1913: 575-579.

78 In Guiard y Larrauri, I, 1913: 579-582.

79 Torres López, 1931: 60.

80 Ordinances of October 22, 1561, on the pilots who carried out their jobs at Portugalete Sandbar, confirmed in 1562. In Guiard y Larrauri, I, 1913: 571-573; Petit, 2016: 147.

81 Ordinances of July 9, 1596, on the rights to be received by the pilots for their work during the entry and exit of Flemish ships in the port of Bilbao. In Guiard y Larrauri, I, 1913: 574-575.

82 Cited in Guiard y Larrauri, I, 1913: 621; and published in Coronas, 1979: 133-135.

83 This ordinance was written in 1669, confirmed in 1672, and amended in 1675. The confirmation of this reform was made in 1677. In Guiard y Larrauri, I, 1913: 621-625.

ordinances were approved, then confirmed in 1688, which dealt with the payment of vouchers and drafts, the organization's doormen, the visits that the consulate authorities had to make to the estuary and the port to verify the condition of the facilities and check the behavior of the officials responsible for their care, the relevant jurisdiction in shipwrecks, and the conditions required of those who offered themselves to hold the most important positions in the institution.[84] And in 1612, 1644, and 1665, further chapters connected with the pilots were dictated.[85]

Apart from the previous ordinances, whose contents were limited to particular matters, in the sixteenth century the consular authorities saw the convenience of forming general, extensive ordinances in order to deal broadly with the issues addressed in the daily operation of the institution and other issues connected with commercial activity. This is the case of those ordinances of 1531, which did not receive

---

84 In Zabala y Allende, 1907: 52-53 and Guiard y Larrauri, I, 1913: 625-629.

85 Petit, 2016: 148.

royal confirmation,[86] and those of 1554 that received the approval of Phillip II in 1560.[87]

The body of consulate ordinances dated in 1531, the institution's first general ones, included forty chapters that dealt with consular offices and jurisdiction, insurance, tariffs, and bills of exchange. While the second round of them, drawn up based on the previous ones from 1531, included more than seventy clauses, and they, too, dealt with elections for consulate positions, the administration of consular justice, and different commercial institutions. In this second text, although it is derived to a large extent from the chapters of 1531, some novelties were incorporated, mainly in relation to tariff rights, insurance contracts, general tariffs, and the registration of goods from the Indies.

This second set of ordinances, confirmed in 1560, are what authors have come to call the "old ordinances" of the Bilbao consulate in order

---

86 In Guiard y Larrauri, I, 1913: 582-598.

87 These ordinances were approved by the Consulate of Bilbao on March 22, 1554, and confirmed by Phillip II on December 15, 1560. As an excerpt they are published in Guiard y Larrauri, I, 1913: 598-621. And they appear in the index in Zabala y Allende, 1907: 109-112.

to contrast them with the "new ordinances"—
those passed in 1737.

The drafting and confirmation of the
ordinances of 1561 did not prevent the
consulate from continuing to draft extensive
new ordinances to reform and complete the
previous ones. However, none of these texts
can have received royal confirmation, which
is why they can never have been more than
simple projects. This must have happened with
those dated February 6, 1588, which had one
hundred seven chapters.[88]

The Successful Ordinances of 1737:
Closer to a Commercial Code than Simple
Corporate Ordinances

At the beginning of the eighteenth century,
the people in charge of the management of the
Consulate of Bilbao considered the possibility of
organizing the institution's regulations (which
had evolved the previous two centuries) because
a very high percentage of the clauses had not
been incorporated into the general ordinances

88 Zabala y Allende, 1907: 19.

confirmed in 1560. Another objective behind this decision was to put into writing the many laws based on custom that were also used within the framework of the consulate—laws passed on by oral transmission that raised serious problems in terms of knowledge, use, and, above all, proof under certain circumstances.

We should add that the consulate must also have known that the monarchy was considering abolishing the institution. So, the consular managers may well have thought that if Madrid tried to do that, it would be better to have their rights properly organized and confirmed as a means of defense. It should be remembered that in 1719, Fortún Íñiguez de Acurio had given the Marquis of Campoflorido his opinion about the possibility of abolishing the Bilbao consulate.[89] Furthermore, the decision to form new ordinances might also have been influenced by the knowledge that Bilbao had (at the beginning of the century) of the ordinances on land and maritime trade passed in France in 1673[90] and

---

89 Zabala y Allende, 1907: 98-100. Íñiguez de Acurio was a representative of the Lordship at court in Madrid when Phillip V was king and the Marquess of Campoflorido finance minister.

90 *Ordonnance de commerce*. March 23, 1673. In Isambert,

1681[91] under the reign of Louis XIV and his powerful minister, Colbert. This knowledge was undoubtedly consolidated if one considers the major presence of French merchants, as well as works on French commercial law, in Bilbao.[92]

The new body of ordinances of the Consulate of Bilbao was confirmed by the monarchy in 1737, concluding the procedure initiated at the end of the previous decade, and for which further texts were drawn up before the definitive chapters of 1737 were written.

At a general meeting held in 1725, the decision was taken to prepare new ordinances that would serve for the resolution of lawsuits and differences that were taken before the consular court for matters of commerce and navigation,[93] a commission being appointed to draft it and be in charge of setting a new system

---

Jourdan, and Decrusy, 19, 1821-1833: 92-107.

91 *Ordonnance de la marine.* Fontainebleau, August 1681. In Isambert, Jourdan, and Decrusy, 19, 1821-1833: 282-366.

92 A forensic allegation with regard to the insurance contract deposited in the Bizkaia government's library (sig. V.f. 2504) expressly states that French ordinances were taken into account in the drafting of the Bilbao regulations. See Petit, 2016: 150, note 23.

93 Zabala y Allende, 1907: 53.

for consular elections and for the administration and payment of damages rights. The result of its activity took shape, at first, in the drafting of a new ordinance approved in 1728, and then in a second text with twenty-six clauses that received confirmation from the monarchy on May 7, 1731.

The result was not to the liking of the institution, which is why the board, on September 13, 1735, again addressed the need to commission the drawing up of new ordinances and decided to delegate to the prior and consuls the appointment of people who could better train them, establishing that expenses arising from that commission would be covered using the ordinary old tariff.[94]

At the general meeting held on September 15, six residents and merchants of the town were appointed to take on the task: Juan Bautista de Guendica y Mendieta, Luis de Ibarra y Larrea, José Manuel de Gorordo, Antonio de Alzaga, José de Zangróniz, and Emeterio de Thelitu.

---

94 Decree of the General Board of Commerce of the Consulate of September 13, 1735. In *Ordenanzas de la Ilustre Universidad y Casa de Contratación*, folios 4-5.

At the same time, the trustee and the secretary of the consulate were at their disposal.[95]

After a little more than a year of work, finally the commissioners presented the text that they had drawn up to the general board of the consulate on December 14, 1736. The chapters, after being reviewed by a group of individuals with knowledge about trade and who met with the editors of the text,[96] were sent to the Council of Castile. The council, after accessing the report presented by Domingo Nicolás Escolano, the king's representative in the Lordship, proceeded to confirm it on December 2, 1737, with only the exception of clause number fifty-four, chapter seventeen, in relation to the wealth of the dowry of wives of the persons or merchants who had gone bankrupt.[97] Then it was put into practice in the

95 Decree of the General Board of Commerce of the Consulate of September 15, 1735. In *Ordenanzas de la Ilustre Universidad y Casa de Contratación*, fol. 5.

96 In addition to the members of the drafting committee, José de Allende Salazar y Cortázar, Ignacio de Barbanchano, Mateo Gómez de la Torre, and José Eguía—residents and merchants of the town—took part in the review. Decree of the General Board of Commerce of the Consulate of December 20, 1736. In *Ordenanzas de la Ilustre Universidad y Casa de Contratación*, fol. 8.

97 The text of confirmation in *Ordenanzas de la Ilustre*

lordship on the eighteenth of the same month, after the Bizkaian authorities had confirmed that the contents of the ordinances were not contrary to the Laws of the Jurisdiction of the Lordship of Bizkaia.[98] It was read and published two days later, according to the customary procedure.[99]

To comply with the order received to form a complete and useful body of ordinances to resolve all issues related to trade, the authors of the chapters took into account the provisions of the Law of July 21, 1494, on the Consulate of Burgos, also applicable to that of Bilbao after its foundation in 1511; the Law of 1511; all the previous ordinances of the institution, in particular the general ones of 1560, as well as those passed in 1672, 1675, 1677, 1688, and 1731; and, finally, "other instruments and papers" and the custom-based law both of the consulate itself and that created by European navigators outside the consulate.[100]

Universidad y Casa de Contratación, fols. 295-297.

98 *Ordenanzas de la Ilustre Universidad y Casa de Contratación*, fols. 298-299.

99 *Ordenanzas de la Ilustre Universidad y Casa de Contratación*, fols. 298-302.

100 *Ordenanzas de la Ilustre Universidad y Casa de*

The result was a very extensive, complete work that far exceeds what had been the consular general ordinances to that date, both in Bilbao and in the other consulates. It does not seem an exaggeration, therefore, to state that the Bilbao consulate's Ordinances of 1737 are closer to a commercial code, such as the French ordinances of 1673 and 1681, than to the body of ordinances of a consular institution, as Zabala y Allende stated at the beginning of the twentieth century.[101]

The work is internally structured into twenty-nine chapters, each divided into a variable number of laws that, together, reach a surprising total of 723. Taking into account the content of the laws, we have identified four main sections. The first one was designed to fix the legal system of the consular institution itself, and the laws of the first eight chapters refer to consular jurisdiction, the offices of the institution, elections, the holding of meetings, the administration of tariffs, and the institution of the trustee. Chapters nine to eighteen deal with the regulation of the institutions of land

Contratación, fols. 9-10.
101 Zabala y Allende, 1907: 80.

trade, including trade books, companies, sale contracts, the commission business, exchange instruments, brokers, and bankruptcies. Chapters nineteen to twenty-four deal with private institutions of commerce by sea, such as the legal system of the charter contract, shipwrecks, ordinary and general tariffs, insurance, bottomry, and personnel of the ships. Finally, the last five chapters deal with port activity on the Bilbao canal, establishing rules to regulate the activity of the main Bilbao pilot, the carpenters-caulkers, bargemen, and boatmen, and the conservation of the estuary.[102]

The text of the ordinances was not to the liking of some merchants from France, Holland, and England, who addressed the monarch and objected to its chapters, to which the monarch responded with a decree of the Council of Castile on December 10, 1740, pointing out that the claimants lacked legitimacy. So, the ordinances had to be complied with and observed.[103]

---

[102] Two summaries of the content of the 723 laws can be seen in Zabala y Allende, 1907: 56-72 and, more recently, in Petit, 2016: 151-158.

[103] In *Ordenanzas de la Ilustre Universidad y Casa de Contratación*, fols. 303-346.

After the Ordinances of 1737 came into force and remained in force until the Bilbao consulate was closed in 1830, replaced by a new commercial court, as had happened with the rest of the state consulates when the Spanish Commercial Code of 1829 took effect with different clauses—some adopted from the consular institution, and others issued by the monarchy introducing some changes to the clauses. Although perhaps the most important reform was that of 1818, the date on which the consulate itself agreed on a series of changes that, passed at the general meeting held on February 8, 1817, were confirmed by Fernando VII on July 9, 1818.[104]

In addition to the breadth of the contents covered by the Ordinances of 1737, which could be considered a commercial code, the text also takes a leading place in the history of commercial law due to its widespread use in both Spain and America. Thus, surpassing the strictly consular and local framework for which they had been intended, they ended up being used within the

---

104 In relation to the modifications made to the Ordinances of 1737 at the initiative of the consulate and the monarchy, see Zabala y Allende, 1907: 72-76.

framework of Spanish-American trade as their chapters were taken as a model for the drafting of the ordinances of other consulates, and as a supplementary right to the norms of others.

In several consulates' foundation certificates (for consulates which, like that of Santander, were set up in the second half of the eighteenth century under the protection of legislation that partially liberalized trade with the Indies) we can see these consulates were expressly subject to the Laws of Castile and the Indies, and to the ordinances in force in the other consulates—in particular those from 1737 of the Consulate of Bilbao.[105]

Likewise, it should be remembered that the management of the Consulate of Donostia took the Bilbao Ordinances of 1737 as a reference for the drafting of its own ones, passed in 1766.[106]

---

105 Among other regulations, it was stipulated in Chapter XLIV of the Creation Certificate of the Consulate of Santander and La Coruña: "For decisions on business that takes place, the consulate will be regulated according to the provisions of the Laws of Castile, and the Indies, and ordinances on the matter, especially that of the Consulate of Bilbao."

106 To see the influence of the Bilbao Ordinances of 1737 on those of the Donostia consulate, see the doctoral thesis of Asier Aritz Arzalluz Loroño, read at the Public University of Navarra in 2017, under the direction of Gregorio Monreal

The Bilbao text also served as a model for the foundation of other bodies of ordinances that were never passed. That is what happened with the draft ordinances for the Santander consulate[107] and for the project that took place in Seville.[108]

In 1808, the Barcelona city council, when requesting a new regulation on commerce, suggested that the drawing up of certain laws on commerce would be simple if the ordinances of consulates were considered, especially those of Bilbao.[109]

Across the Atlantic, the Bilbao Ordinances of 1737 influenced the law of various American consulates, such as those of Buenos Aires and Mexico.[110] And in North America, at the time of establishing the sources for the legal system in

Zia and Margarita Serna Vallejo, with the title: *Historical-institutional studies of the Consulate of San Sebastián (1682-1829)*. The text of the thesis can be consulted in the repository of the Public University of Navarra at: https://academica-e.unavarra.es/xmlui/handle/2454/32163.

107 Serna Vallejo, 2012: 113.

108 Heredia Herrera, 1970: 230.

109 Quote found in Petit, 2016: 161.

110 On the influence that the Bilbao ordinances had in Latin America, see Divar, 2007.

force in Louisiana after its purchase, an 1806 ruling from the Legislative Council of the Territory of Orleans established that "in matters of commerce the ordinance of Bilbao is that with full authority."[111]

The general recognition of the seniority and credit of the Consulate of Bilbao, and of the authority of the Ordinances of 1737 throughout the monarchy, justified Charles IV granting the Consulate of Bilbao the status of *Lordship* in 1791.[112]

Finally, a major part of the Bilbao consulate ordinances became more widely valid in 1805 once they were partly incorporated into the *Novísima Recopilación* passed for the whole of the monarchy.

After 1830, the history of the Consulate of Bilbao and its admired Ordinances of 1737 ended, but the memory and recollection of what they meant for Bilbao, for the Lordship of Bizkaia, and for the monarchy itself, has lasted over time in a way that the captains, shipmasters, merchants, and traffickers of Bilbao who began

---

111 Donlan, 2014: 225-226.

112 Guiard y Larrauri, II, 1913: 608-609.

to fight for the foundation of the consulate in 1495 would never have imagined, and which, over the following centuries, contributed decisively to the formation of commercial law that ended up going far beyond the strictly local, consular framework for which it had been designed.

Bibliography

Arzalluz Loroño, Asier Aritz (2017). *Institutional legal study of the Consulate of San Sebastián (1682-1829)*, read at the Public University of Navarra under the direction of Gregorio Monreal Zia and Margarita Serna Vallejo. The thesis can be consulted in the repository of this university: https://hdl.handle.net/2454/32163.

Basas Fernández, Manuel (1963). *El Consulado de Burgos en el siglo XVI*, Madrid: Consejo Superior de Investigaciones Científicas-Escuela de Historia Moderna; (1994) Facsimile edition, Burgos: Diputación Provincial de Burgos

Benito y Endara, Lorenzo (1896). *Ensayo de una introducción al estudio del derecho mercantil (preliminares e historia)*. Valencia: Imprenta de F. Domenech.

Blanco Constans, Francisco (1895-1897). *Estudios elementales de derecho mercantil sobre la filosofía, la historia y la legislación positiva*. Granada: *Revista General de Legislación y Jurisprudencia*.

Consulado, y Casa de la Contratación de la M.N. y M. L. Ciudad de San Sebastián, y Ordenanzas, con que se debe gobernar, confirmadas por el Real, y Supremo

Consejo de Castilla, segunda impresión. San Sebastián: Pedro de Vgartee, 1714.

Coronas González, Santos Manuel (1979). "La jurisdicción mercantil castellana en el siglo XVI", in Santos Manuel Coronas González, *Derecho mercantil castellano. Dos estudios históricos.* León: Universidad de León, pp. 9-169.

Diccionario marítimo español, que además de las definiciones de las voces con sus equivalentes en francés, inglés e italiano, contiene tres vocabularios de estos idiomas en las correspondencias castellanas. Redactado por orden del Rey nuestro Señor, Madrid, Imprenta Real, 1831.

Divar, Javier (2007). *El Consulado de Bilbao y la extensión americana de sus Ordenanzas de comercio (500 aniversario: 1511-2011).* Madrid: Dykinson / Cámara de Comercio de Bilbao.

Donlan, Sean Patrick (2014). "Entangled up in Red, White, and Blue: Spanish West Florida and the American Territory of Orleans, 1803-1810", in Thomas Duve (ed.), *Entanglements in Legal History: Conceptual Approaches*, Frankfurt am Main: Max Planck Institute for European Legal History, pp. 213-252.

Enríquez Fernández, Javier, Concepción Hidalgo de Cisneros Amestoy, Adela Martínez

Lahidalga (1999a), *Colección documental del Archivo Histórico de Bilbao (1300-1473)*, San Sebastián: Eusko Ikaskuntza (Society for Basque Studies).

——— (1999b). *Colección documental del Archivo Histórico de Bilbao (1473-1500)*, San Sebastián: Eusko Ikaskuntza (Society for Basque Studies).

——— (2000). *Documentary collection of the Bilbao Historical Archive (1501-1514)*, San Sebastián: Eusko Ikaskuntza (Society for Basque Studies).

Gaclo Fernández, Enrique (1971). *Historia de la jurisdicción mercantil en España*. Seville: Universidad de Sevilla.

García de Quevedo y Concellón, Eloy (1905). *Ordenanzas del Consulado de Burgos de 1538 que ahora de nuevo se publican, anotadas, y precedidas de un bosquejo histórico del Consulado*. Burgos: Imprenta de la Diputación.

García Fernández, Ernesto (2005). "The merchant guilds, Basque mareantes and fishermen in the Middle Ages", in Beatriz Arízaga and Jesús Solórzano Telechea (coordinators). *Cities and port towns of the Atlantic in the Middle Ages. Nájera. Encuentros Internacionales del Medievo. Nájera, July 27-30, 2004*, Logroño: Instituto de Estudios Riojanos, pp. 257-294.

García Sanz, Arcadio (1969). "Influencia de los Consulados de mar de Barcelona y Valencia en la erección del Consulado de Burgos (1494)", in *Boletín de la Sociedad Castellonense de Cultura*, 45: 225-244.

González Arce, José Damián (2009). "La ventaja de llegar primero. Estrategias en la pugna por la supremacía mercantil durante los inicios de los Consulados de Burgos y Bilbao (1450-1515)", in *Miscelánea Medieval Murciana*, 33: 77-97.

——— (2010). "La Universidad de mercaderes de Burgos y el Consulado castellano en Brujas durante el siglo XV", in *En la España medieval*, 33: 161-202.

——— (2019). "Los inicios de la Universidad de mercaderes de Bilbao (1481-1511). Corporación de representación gremial e institución de gobierno portuario", in *Studia Historica. Historia Medieval*, 37-1: 187-206.

Guiard y Larrauri, Teófilo (1913). *Historia del Consulado y Casa de Contratación de Bilbao y del comercio de la villa. I. (1511-1699). II. (1700-1830)*. Bilbao: Imprenta y Librería de José de Astuy.

Gumuzio Añibarro, Miren Edurne (2017). *Las ordenanzas del Consulado de Bilbao: su régimen jurídico y proyección internacional en el marco de la Historia del Derecho mercantil europeo entre los siglos XIV y XIX.* Doctoral thesis.

Heredia Herrera, Antonia (1970). "Apuntes para la historia del Consulado de la Universidad de Cargadores a Indias en Sevilla y Cádiz", in *Anuario de Estudios Americanos,* 27: 219-279.

Isambert, F. A., A. J. L. Jourdan, and Decrusy (1821-1833). *Recueil général des anciennes lois françaises depuis l'an 420 jusqu'à la Révolution de 1789.* [29 vols.]. París: Librairie de Plon Frères.

Mut Remola, Elías (1952). "Notas sobre la vida económica de Lérida", in *Instituciones económicas, sociales y políticas de la época fernandina. V Congreso de Historia de la Corona de Aragón.* Zaragoza: Institución Fernando el Católico, pp. 53-76.

Olaran Múgica, Clotilde (2011). "El Consulado de Bilbao y sus ordenanzas. Ordenanzas manuscritas e impresas", in *Boletín Jado,* 22: 265-270.

Ordenanzas de la Ilustre Universidad y Casa de Contratación de la M.N. y M. L. Villa de Bilbao, (insertos sus reales privilegios) aprobadas y confirmadas por el Rey Nuestro Señor Don Phelipe Quinto (que Dios guarde). Año de 1737. Madrid: Oficina de D. Pedro Marín, 1787.

Ordenanzas para el prior y cónsules de la universidad de los mercaderes de la ciudad de Sevilla. Sevilla: Joseph de Blàs y Quesada, 1739.

Petit, Carlos (2016). *Historia del Derecho mercantil.* Madrid: Marcial Pons.

Prematicas, ordenanças, ley, y facultad dada por sus Magestades por Priuilegio especial, a la vniuersidad de la contratacion de los fiel, y Consules de la muy noble vila de Bilbao, Las. Alcalá de Henares: 1552.

Salazar Arechalde, José Ignacio (2003) "Gobierno local en el Bilbao bajomedieval, *Bidebarrieta,*" in *Revista de Humanidades y Ciencias Sociales de Bilbao,* 12: 183-197.

Serna Vallejo, Margarita (2012). "Las cédulas de creación de los Consulados de Santander y La Coruña: el soporte jurídico para la incorporación de las oligarquías locales a los nuevos Consulados", in Manuel Estrada Sánchez y Manuel Artaza Montero (eds.), *Entre Monarquía y Nación. Galicia, Asturias y Cantabria (1700-1833).* Santander: Ediciones de la Universidad de Cantabria, pp. 91-114.

——— (2014). "El bicentenario de la muerte de Antonio de Capmany y Montpalau: una oportunidad para el estudio del derecho marítimo y del Consulado de Barcelona de la Baja Edad Media a la segunda mitad del siglo XVIII", in *Initium*, 19: 711-776.

――― (2018a). *Textos jurídicos marítimos medievales*. Madrid: BOE.

――― (2018b). "Los Consulados del mar aragoneses y castellanos: diferencias y similitudes como resultado de un análisis comparado", in Ramón Lanza García (coordinador), *Las instituciones económicas, las finanzas públicas y el declive de España en la Edad Moderna*. Madrid: UAM Ediciones, pp. 315-344.

Smith, Robert Sidney (1978). *Historia de los Consulados de Mar (1250-1700)*. Barcelona: Ediciones Península.

Torres López, Manuel (1931). "El proceso de formación de las Ordenanzas de Bilbao de 1737", in Teófilo Guiard y Larrauri, Manuel Torres López, Antonio Elias y Suárez, *Las Ordenanzas del Consulado de Bilbao. Tres conferencias con motivo de centenario de su derogación*. Bilbao: Escuelas Gráficas de la Santa Casa de la Misericordia, pp. 40-72.

Zabala y Allende, Federico (1907). *El Consulado y las ordenanzas de comercio de Bilbao con breves noticias históricas del comercio de esta villa*. Bilbao: Imp. y Enc. La Editorial Vizcaína.

Made in the USA
Monee, IL
25 March 2022

92920927R00066